Changing Seasons

Changing Seasons

A Poetic Journey Over Three Continents

H. C. Kim

Writers Club Press
San Jose New York Lincoln Shanghai

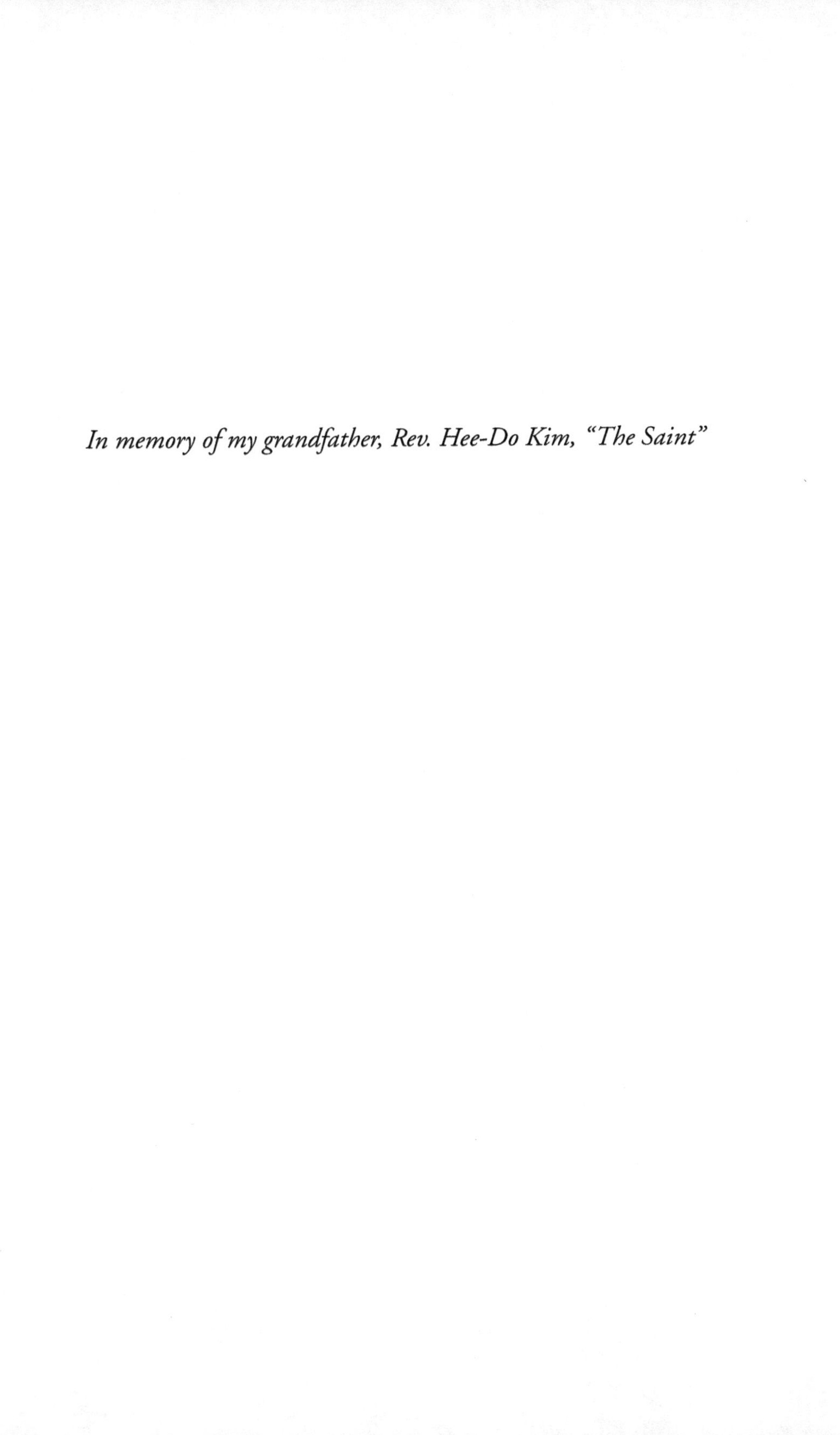

In memory of my grandfather, Rev. Hee-Do Kim, "The Saint"

Preface

Poems contained in this collection testify to a year long effort on my part to capture the essence of the human experience through poetry. Some of the poems are based on real places and concrete experiences; others were composed in the spirit of creative artistic exercise. But they all touch upon important aspects of the human experience, such as love, freedom, and social justice. Most of the poems were written from the fall season of 1999 to the fall season of 2000. And they were all written in one of three places: the English University town of Cambridge, historically eventful Jerusalem, and Providence, Rhode Island. I hope that you will enjoy your poetic journey through changes in seasons over three continents.

H. C. Kim
Advent 2000
Jesus College
Cambridge

"The Flower"

With a slight wave
Beckons the red flower by the windowsill
Come! The warmth of Jerusalem's summer breeze
Enwrap me in your gentle embrace
Caress me with the fingers
That have stroked the timeless city walls
Embrace me with the arms
That have softly held the Tower of David
Release me not from the sweet intimacy
That whispers Jerusalem's fascination

"A Jog in the Streets of Bar Kochba"

In the Streets of Bar Kochba
My steps cautiously touch the long side walk
Slowly bending slightly curving
All the while a smooth journey
Leaves fluttering gently caressing
I pause to look at a leaf
Inaudibly kissing a side of a tree
As it makes its path towards the side walk
A whiff of wind
Sublime scent of the morning air
Elates my light heart
My heart races
As I start my jog
My steps embracing the gently turning side walk
The golden morning sun
Colors the morning path
Warms my body
Slowly drops of sweat touches the side walk
A path that came to be familiar
To my lasting jog

"A Rainy Day in Jerusalem"

Flowing down the street
In a trickle in a gentle flow
On a day
The sun refuses to share
Greets the flowing
Stream from above
In a winter eve
A day for rain
To partake
Of its share
A need
A greeting
Joy for all
Life!
How precious are the drops
That embrace the Jerusalem streets

"A Walk on Mount Scopus"

Today's quiet warmth of the afternoon rays
Radiates and refreshes
As I surrender to the balmy Jerusalem breeze
Calling softly for a short respite
Yearning to aid to renew
That of yesterdays
Hope of the past
Owing tomorrows
Resonance
Promise
Exuberance

"Melek Ha-Falafel"

In the streets of King George
Walking up the gentle hill
To a place quite familiar
Fragrant is the reward
Extending its delight
Down the hill below
Expectant
Hopeful
Forward
Awaits a mouthful
Of that Jerusalem falafel

"Grandma's Love"

Bustling crowd
All around
My hand
Firmly in her hand
Clasped
As if life depended on it

You are my life
I adore you
My grandson
I would see the proclamation
In her gentle gaze

In the turmoil of shopping frenzy
A corner of peace and love
A centrifugal force
Making the world go around and around
My world

Walking past the fish section
Splashing
Live fish assert their existence
Odors of the sea encapsulated within

Fighting their last good fight
I know
I can be that strong
With grandma by my side

Crab, here, Crab!
Very fresh
And delicious
With the best price of the season!
I would buy a dozen if you give me a discount
Okay
You are special so I will give you a small discount

In the midst of buying and selling
Transactions for profit and gain
Exists
Love
Freely given
With no self-interest
Just given
The love of grandma
To her grandson

"Questions"

————— ∞ —————

Can I run faster than the train, dad?
I will try
Quickly
I run through the middle isle
Smiling

We are headed to grandma's, right dad?
I am going to count
Continually
I sit and look at the watch
Expectant

Grandma's going to make her tasty soup, dad?
I think
Wonderfully
I know that it is going to taste
Content

Grandma loves her little grandson, doesn't she dad?
I remember
Sweetly
I went to the Pusan Seafood Market with my hand in hers
Firmly

Grandma is going to live forever, isn't she dad?
I learned
Yesterday
I learned that those who love God, like my grandma, lives
Forever

"A Piece of Heaven"

River flowing through the city
Seems to have captured a piece of heaven
Colors of blue sky
Find kinship in the blueness of the vibrant stream
Even the night sky is represented in the late afternoon water flow
Like the stars in heaven
Glisten bits of sunrays hitting against constantly moving water mass
That constellation over there looks like the Milky Way pictures I have
seen
This surely could pass for the Little Dipper

Standing above the water sky
On a stone bridge hewn by human hands
I find myself
Losing myself
In the imaginary celestial world
Projected on the rushing waters below
Somehow I forget the reality
And start dreaming of the future
The possibilities
That might at first seem ephemeral
And unattainable
In the real world

But just as the heaven
Created on the water below
Is so real to me
I find assurance
As I gaze upon the constructed reality
Of the future
That holds promise and redemption

With this hope
I continue my late afternoon walk
Looking up at the sky
Knowing that soon
It will be night
And the sky will be filled with stars
Brightly shining
Even brighter than the stars
That I have seen on the waters

"A School of Small Fish"

On a quaint bridge
I stand and look towards the cascade
Of rushing waters nearby
From the top of the rocky hill
To the bottom of the waterfall
Flowing towards the pond in a distance

In the midst of the live
Effervescent waters
A school of small fish
Strives against the current
Even towards the bottom of the harsh waterfall

For what purpose
I cannot fathom
It surely is not for baptism under running water
As the early Christian teaching document
The Didache dictates for new believers

Perhaps
This gives a sense of being alive
Going against the current
Struggling to achieve

And survive
Like pinching oneself to know that one is not dreaming
Swimming towards a difficult direction
Feeling the pain of it all
Knowing that each stride accomplished
Is a true feat
Of much effort

I do see some things going with the current
Broken off branches
Perhaps from a tree branch that wandered towards the waterfall
And with a slightly more extended reach became cut off
Also leaves which have fallen off with the passage of time
Dead fish as well
Which might have given up the struggle to survive against the currents
Not being able to reach its paradise
Filled with fish food and a resting place
All these flow down the river towards the pond below
Soon they leave my vision
But the school of fish struggling
Appear prominent
Alive
Full of hope and promise

I find myself rooting for the school of fish
Making only a little progress with the passage of time
Swimming against a strong and powerful wave
Surely they will reach their goal
And find satisfaction
Rest

"A Single Red Leaf"

Drifting along
A bright red leaf
Turns this way
And that
As if to show off its most glorious color
The very best view
Almost leaping along
In its levity
And glorious frolic

I come to a standstill
Almost awed by the gall
Bravado of this beautiful leaf
So much confidence
As if its existence matters most
Well
I did come to admire it
It did turn my course
Certainly
There is importance for me
Of this red leaf

Gazing upon
The playful gait
Of the red leaf
I cannot help but want to reach out
And feel a part of the life
Of the red leaf
Seemingly
Beckoning me to follow

That which is all around me
Takes backstage
As the red leaf captures my vision
And I find my steps moving towards the
Mesmerizing leaf
Independent
By now
Gently flying
As I extend my hand
With steps hurrying towards it
The red leaf seems to turn around
And begin to amble towards me

Suddenly
With an element of surprise
The beautiful red leaf
Falls into my hand
Completely open to receive
A smile finds its way into my face
And my heart feels lighter
It's amazing
What a single red leaf
Can bring

"From the Pink Bowl"

From the pink bowl
Comes the fragrance of
The rose garden
How could such a small bowl capture the essence of a gigantic rose
garden?
But surely it does
And as I smell the colorful odors emanating from
The pink bowl
I trace my memory back to the day I spent walking along the rose gar-
den
Even within it
Fields laden with roses of all kinds
Flagrance that captured many people's heart
And my fascination
The sheer beauty of the flowers
Coupled with their scent
Was certainly a combination
Quite impossible to resist
I look at the contents of the flower bowl before me
Within it I see a collection of flowers
That have served their visitors well in their life time
Still carrying on the fragrance that marked the beauty of their life time
Even though now dried up

Unplanted from their home ground
Displaced from their beautiful flower vase on the coffee table
They retain their original hue
Although brightness of their original color gone
They have certainly retained the sweet aroma of their former years
Now providing a piece of nature
And heaven's beauty
On my desk
And giving me the gift and pleasure of
Their scent

"Glowing Walls"

Walking along the street by the moonlight
As night brightness dawns on the garden walls
I notice white walls with a certain ephemeral glow
Passing by me in the other direction
In the darkening evening mist
All else fade into the background
Cars parked along the street
Trees on the other side of the street
Houses on either side
And even occasional bicycles passing by
But the swiftly passing white walls
Some of them smooth in surface
Others slightly rough on the edges
Even with almost a deliberate imbalance
They all glow beautifully under the stars
Occasionally
Leaves and tree branches
Which succeeded in extending their reach
From within the house garden
Touch my shoulder or my upper arm
While clinging to the walls that prohibit their free outgrowth
I feel an impulse to push the leaves away
Although they are harmless

And certainly not unpleasant to the touch
I walk swiftly
Thinking about the final destination
Where surprises await
Or at least hope for beautiful surprises
Now
Somehow
I begin to smell the flowers
And the sweet evening atmosphere
Glowing walls beginning to fade into the background

"Like A Gardener"

Softly
On the green grass
I tread my steps
Walking
Gently stepping
Careful to preserve the seemly pristine beauty that I see
As if heavy steps would affect the very aesthetics of the form
It does feel good to revel in the beauty of nature before me
I have admired from afar looking at the perfect patch of grass
So evergreen
Symmetric as can be
Now partaking of its wonderful offering
Feeling like a part of it
I find myself wanting to preserve its nature
What makes it so wonderful to behold
Thus
Gently I traverse
The domesticated field around me
Feeling like a gardener

"Nature's Beautiful Masterpiece"

Behind the green wall
Of living matter
So nicely trimmed and groomed
That it attests to the beauty of human garden art
Sway tall trees
To and fro
Free as birds
Wild in their growth
Not managed by professional gardeners
But from this angle
They all blend into
Beautiful greenery

Behind the trees
Clouds have formed a white canvas background
With beautiful variation of the white color
I think I even see white with blue mixed in
And the sun trying to shine through
Adds ethereal element
Almost adding an outer world feel

The real eye catcher
Of course

Is in the foreground
Violet flowers
Dancing to nature's music
Inaudible to human ears
With the encouragement of nature's wind
Moving from side to side
Even jumping up and down
At times
At least it seems to me
They certainly are beautiful

Nature's beautiful masterpiece
Is framed as a vertical triptych
By my window panes
And crimson curtains
Add a royal element to the beautiful view
Somehow
It seems appropriate

"Pebbles"

Pebbles here
Pebbles there
Right in front of me
Almost touching my feet
But not quite
As I sit on a bench
Made of stone
Underneath an umbrella
Made of leaves
Luscious green
Attached to a big tree
Arching over me
Almost enfolding me in its midst
I take a bite of my sandwich
With a singular bite
I notice a lone bee flying closer in
Remembering being stung by a bee just several days ago
I eye the bee carefully
As if my gaze would turn its course
The bee settles on one of the leaves
Surely no interest in stinging me
I continue my gaze
Wondering this time

Why a bee sits there and walks on that leaf
It's not a flower
There surely is no honey
Slightly doubtful I take a leaf
Close by
To examine it
No odor of sweetness there
But the bee lingers
Walks on the leaf
Soon enough
Another bee joins
Flying in
Takes possession of the leaf right next door
There must be something that attracts these bees
Utterly confounded
Not knowing what could be the factor
I gaze down again at the pebbles
Right near my feet
They are arranged along the edges of a nice patch of green grass
In fact
I could see that the pebbles are imbedded onto the floor
Basically framing the large grass rectangle
I continue looking at the pebble frame
Being intrigued by it
Quickly I find myself being gazed upon by the two bees
Who seemed amazed that I am looking at the imbedded pebbles
Rather than the vibrant
Nicely tailored
Green grass

"Sheep"

Sheep
Gathered in two's and three's
To the right
And to the left
On green grass patches
And even some ambulating
On the path made for people
And cars

Quietly they stand there
Thinking about something
Perhaps just enjoying a nice
Fall sunshine
And fresh countryside air
Probably not wanting interruption
Of their pastime

Unwittingly
We approach
Thinking to befriend these lovely creatures
Walking softly towards them
Unaware of any invitation or lack thereof
Which their sheep body language exuded

Perhaps curiosity played a role
How would they feel?

One of us steps on their excrement
But ignoring a possible cosmic sign
We joke and traverse towards the sheep mini-herd
We feel accomplishment with each step
As sheep stand unmoved
But there is distance still
Sure enough
As we close in
Closer to the white fur balls
So fuzzy looking
Only a few steps in distance
They move away
Without even turning their heads
With direction and purpose
Namely
That of moving away from us

We are forgiving
Of their rejection
After all
They are sheep
And we were the ones who disturbed

From a distance
We continue our appreciation
In our near proximity
Sheep in two's and three's
And in the distance
A whole herd of sheep

Color the countryside
Covering quite a bit of the green grass
So characteristic of these beautiful parts

Soon
We approach the front entrance
Of the building
Where no sheep is allowed
We turn back
To see our sheep friends
Just once more

Then we enter
The place of
Human
Privilege

"The Big Tree"

Standing here
In front of the big tree
I find myself less than one fourth in width of the tree
It sure is a different picture
Than when I used to look at this tree from a distance
It always looked so small
So insignificant
But up close
I find myself awed by its size
I want a recording of some sort
Perhaps in remembrance
Or for proof of the tree size
I don't exactly know
But I do certainly find myself
Asking a friend to take a picture of me
Standing right in front of the tree
My back literally touching the tree
To show the scale difference as accurately as possible
As my friend backs up
I remind her to back up enough
To include the whole size of the tree in the picture
I know
I will look like an ant in the picture

My face hardly to be seen
I tell her
Tree size is what I want captured in the picture
As my friend backs up
With the camera pressed against her eye
I find myself thinking
About the age of the tree
It must have lived a long life given its size
In what historical events it might have served as a prop
What lovers shared their first kiss under this very tree
As I allow my thoughts to wander
My friend tells me that she can now frame the picture
In the way she wants
Although I know that smiling for the camera
Might be fruitless given how small I will look in the picture
I smile any way
Probably out of habit
As my friend presses the shutter button
I wonder
How old I am in tree years

"The Silver Thread"

———— ∞ ————

A strand of silver string
Loudly glistening on a tree
In the midst of fluttering green leaves
Barely thin lines protruding from slightly thicker branches
Though not a pine tree
Must be of the same family group
Perhaps with a similar Latin name
Quite different
However
In this tree's directionless protrusion
Leave antennas extending in every direction
As if to seek different sources of energy and resources
Although air is same all around
It is true
Some leaves are optimized
For greatest time in sunshine warmth

In the midst of multiplicity of green lines
Occupying a corner space in the garden
Shines a silver line
Reflecting the sunlight
Relaying sun's glory
Almost brighter than a mirror catching a sunshine ray

With each wind blow
Flashing more poignantly
Than a camera flash
What is this silver thread
Catching my eye?
The pink flowers
So beautiful in their form
All around the garden
Prominently standing
Capture no such interest

Then comes the realization
The sliver thread
Is a piece of thin branch
Even broken
Drooping down from its mother branch

"UFO"

Drops of rain cling to my window
Providing a prism of sorts to view the outside world
Through a rain drop
Glued to the window glass
I look out
Blurry glob of green is all I see through the small portal
I draw myself back
From my close proximity to the window
My nose almost as red as Rudolf's
From having touched the cool window glass
I take a wider view through the window
And see before me the beauty of the green
Unidentified Fuzzy Objects
My UFO
Is now a clear picture of the beauty that exists
Less than a stone's throw away
Through the clearly rain trodden landscape
I see the beauty of the trees
Flowers
And luscious green grass
All of which
Inevitably needs the water

Which it received this morning
And days before
To thrive

"We Are All Flowers"

Drops of rain
Rushing down onto the pavement
I could hear the rain droplets hitting the ground
Flowing like a small stream
Waters from above make their way onto the ground below
A small stream of water has made its own course
Towards the patch of grass in a short distance
I see the clear green colors of the grass
That is receiving its surfeit of heavenly waters

As I step out of my warm hall way
Past the front door
I feel what I see
As rain drops hit my hair
My arms
And my ears

I hear a different sound as the drops hitting the pavement before me
Rain becomes alive to me
And I feel more than hear
As the rain drops
Provide a contrast and a new experience
From the warmth that I have felt in my room

The world has renewed
Is renewing
In the cycle of water
Going from earth to heaven
And then from heaven to earth
I feel essentially a part of that
As I receive my portion of heavenly blessing
For without water
Can I behold the beauty of the fall flowers?
My substance itself is dependent on it
Like a flower
I consume my share of water
From the water cycle
And I know that who I am
What I am
Glows in beauty for someone to behold
And enjoy

We are all flowers
Making our way in this world
Bringing joy to someone out there

"A Picture Perfect"

In the midst of rolling trees
And overflowing ferns
Colored in green
Ranging from bright and variegated even to dark green
Neighboring trees with red leaves
Almost purple in color
Planted here and there
Visibly in the midst of all the green
Nonetheless harmoniously forming an idyllic picture
In the natural canvas
So pleasant and soothing to the sight

Over the grouped leaves
Wrapped by tree branches and
Aesthetically tangled in green web of splendid colors
Diversity of hues sprinkled over their form
Whitish pink flowery confetti nature-born
Arches gently in waves
Like a string of popcorn
Adorning a Christmas tree
But more gracefully
Even tastier
Certainly to my eyes

In fact
Everything that is above level ground
Seems wholeheartedly adorned by natural delight
Verdant and glowing
Picturesque more than the pictures that I have seen in a nature maga-
zine
Without wearing a three dimensional lens
Like in I-Max theaters with pictures that jump out at you
I behold
A beautiful patch of ebullient green grass
Reaching out towards me
As if extending greetings from the green vines along the wall
In a short distance
Next to the neighboring buildings

What a picture of beauty
Right here in the backyard

"A Week Of Festivities"

Winds are blowing
This cool evening
Early night air
Fresh as can be
From the morning
Showers
With additional afternoon rains
In the calmness of this night
Only disturbance is that of the frolicking gale
Blowing
Well groomed
Beautiful hair
To and fro
Extracting a gentle
But playful smile
Ruffling a well situated garment
Perhaps providing a slight discomfort
This could be a good thing…
The night in anticipation
Of something
It is a week of festivities
To celebrate Halloween
Perhaps something supernatural

Or magical may happen
In a beautiful night like this
Spark of something greater than the visible world
May be a type of reformation
After all
Some will celebrate the Reformation Day
The same day as the Halloween
A personal reformation
And change
Could possibly be
With willingness to hold onto something larger than self
Alacrity to seize something
Even making oneself vulnerable
Such reformation of sorts
Is certainly possible in a magical night like this
Winds travel past
By me
Tenderly
But with certainty
Heralding the possibilities

"The Rose Garden"

Brightly shining under the sun
Myriad of colors carpet the garden floor
Bright pink
Royal Red
White
Yellow
All shapes and sizes
With fragrance sweeter than the choice of perfumes

As I walk around the circular rose garden
Divided into different colored rose sections
I contemplate different stages in my life
My birth
Childhood
Teenage years
And young adulthood
Somehow my life does not seem so neatly arranged
Nor particularly odoriferous as this garden
But certainly more colorful

Paths treaded in no linear way
Had their own system
And direction

Experiences garnered along the way
Have enriched and educated
Indeed
Like a pastiche of beautiful roses in a garden
In my eyes
My life has its beauty
So I am proud to be the owner of a beautiful garden
One that is called
My life

"The Winding Path Along The Lake"

A winding path along a lake
Lined with trees
Both big and small
Narrow and wide
Even bamboo shoots
Which are really grass
And of course
Green grass as well
All over the hills to the right
To the left
Nice patches of grass by the water bank

Beneath me
I see fallen leaves
Some trampled on all day long
Others
Freshly fell
Mixed with dropped berries
And nuts
I search for the source of these fruits of the earth
And find them hanging plentifully
All around me

Not knowing whether
Edible or not
I hesitate
Soon
I am directed to berries
Good to consume
Freshly plucked from their place
Also to nuts
This time
Picked from the ground
Where they fell from branches up high
Then unshelled
Both sublime to the taste

I take a whiff of the fresh air
As if I could capture the spirit of this place
This way
The path by the lake
Beautiful trees all around
And the taste of earth goodies
I feel successful
For I feel good

I take to steps again
Before me
A road lined with
Berries and nuts
Beautifully colored leaves
Trees to greet me at each step
And green grass adding to nature's beauty
In jubilation
I amble along
The winding path along the lake

"Bike Path"

The path
Leading to the
Waters
Glistening
In the autumn dusk

A road through
The neighborhood
Marked
By history and tradition

Over the bridge
Picturesque
Like the ones
In the Hallmark movies

To the side
An American Tourister factory
Having their annual year end clearance sale
A mark of labor force in this town

Little beyond
On the other side

Closer to the waters
Stands the German club
A testimony to the immigrant residents

Riding my bicycle
Sailing through the gentle winds
Appreciating
The beauty of Warren

Life seems complete
Not because everything is okay
It is the simple pleasure
Of a fall bike ride
Little things
Bring big significance

"An autumn basketball game"

Before me
Lies the street
Beautifully marked
With autumn facade
Of multicolored leaves

Yet
What I see
Lies beyond
Further beyond
In
Time

My thoughts race
Past
Several
Passed autumn seasons
To a distant
Memory

One fall day
Many years ago,
I remember

Playing
One
On
One
Rough house basketball

I had never met the challenger before
And the gentle ambiance of the fall
Seemed to discourage
A rigorous duel of basketball

I took the challenge anyway
Serious expression
A slight friendly smile
But the competition was set

Vigorously
Rigorously
Running
To
And
Fro

Basketball
Flying
Hookshot
Layup
A three pointer
Albeit played by street rules

A refreshing game
Active as can be

As if all was on the line

After an hour
Rivalry
Turns to friendship
Next time
We'll have another rigorous game
That's for sure

How simply frienships were formed
In that autumn day
In Philadelphia
City of
Brotherly love

So many autumn seasons past

"*Golden Leaf*"

Softly fluttering in the wind
Gently rolling along the hillside
Hopping off the beaten path
Is a blonde
Leaf
Fresh off the autumn tree

Searching for something?
Merely frolicking in the glorious Fall?
Asserting her independence?

Freely she runs, rolls, and flies
As if there's no worry in the world
As if the world is a big blank canvas
And her each imprint
Glorious masterpiece

"Autumn Hill"

Slowly the hillside comes into focus
into sharp focus
of autumn
Impressionism

Red, orange, yellow, fading green
Leaves in their full glory
Even shading the three trunks
And branches
Brown hardly to be seen

From the station of
Providence
As the trains hug their tracks
And shouting in glorious ecstasy
A view of the Hill
With its own natural enthusiasm
Of the Fall

"Holding onto the Fall"

In the streets of Providence
Shouts Providence
Seemingly
It is the time for Fall

Season for changes
Colors of the Leaves
Soon to Leave their nesting place
Still to indulge in the pleasure of the Fall

Too early to be cast out
Holding on to their Branches
Branching out to face the gentle gale
Enwrapped in the pleasure of the sun of the Fall

"Changes"

Falling upon a pile of the autumn leaves
Raked to the side
Looking this way and that
Can't have anyone see a grown person
Frolicking in the pleasure of the Fall

But why not?
Wasn't small pleasures such as these that made me happy?
That made others who are just as grown up as I am happy once?
Fall is a season of changes
But the Fall is everlastingly the same
The Leaves change color
Beautify and glorify the Nature
And they fall
To be raked

It is not Fall that has changed
It is not Fall that testify best to the changes in life
Is it not us
We ourselves best testify to changes
When small pleasures that once made us happy
Becomes a social crime of sorts

Looking this way and that
I try to capture the simple pleasures in Life
As the Fall remains

"What is Fall?"

Fall is not
Is Too
Nope
Yes it is

Fall is
Not so
Sure it is
Certainly an impossibility

What is
Not that it is
Could it be
Can't be

"Fall Confession"

———— ∞ ————

Tenderness is what I seek
Said she in the autumn twilight
Gentleness
And sweetness

As leaves fell in the distance
Said he
You are whom I want
You are my Tenderness
You are my Gentleness
You are my Sweetness
You are my All

"Apple Picking"

Baskets filled with apples
Friends tossing an apple to and fro
As if tossing a baseball
But without the glove
Look at that apple
Way up there
Can you get it for me?
No why don't you get it!
Here's the ladder
Okay
Let me climb up
What a glorious apple!
Plucked right off the tree
Can't wait to taste its juices
With each bite
There will surely be pleasure
Nothing like a fresh apple
Picked on a beautiful autumn day

"Hope"

———— ∞ ————

Lying on the bed of
Natural Impressionism
Of beautifully colored leaves

I paint an impressionist masterpiece of my own
In the sky
Hardly blemished by a single passing cloud

What was was
What is is
And what will be will be

No!
What was was
What is can be
What will be surely will be

"Lone Red Leaf"

———— ∞ ————

Walking along the park
I couldn't help
But to pick up a lone
Red Leaf among the golden ones

I don't know why I felt compelled
I was hurrying to the library

Perhaps I thought that the Leaf could make a good bookmark
But I have tons of free bookmarks from Amazon.com

Perhaps I wanted a memory of this year's fall
No, I am not so sentimental in that way
After all, how many leaves did I collect to commemorate previous Falls?

Could it be because of the beauty
One sees in uniqueness
Individuality
A self-assertiveness
Of a lone
Red Leaf
Among all the golden ones?

Could it be because I want to be like that Leaf?

"Leaves are falling"

Leaves are falling
Gently
Riding down the
Cascading gale
Fluttering in the last grasp of being airborn
Soon to rest in the ground
Never to know the heights again
To be trampled
To be crushed

Leaves are falling
In droves
It's merely the time for their fall
After a fruitful greenery
Transitioning into glorious colors
Yellow
Red
Orange
Time to come down to the ground below

Leaves are falling
Inevitable
Cycle of history

Origin
Climax
Fall
It is destiny
A fact of life
The fall reminds

"*Winter is coming*"

---∞---

Snow will soon cover the branches
Winter winds will enwrap me in its embrace
Leaves will soon be no more
People will no longer behold with amazement
The beauty of my splendor
Leaves brightly shining

Spring flowers surrounding my base
With fragrance beyond words
Summer sunrays warming
My very being
Fall breeze slightly
Teasing me
No more
Winter will surely come

Memories will remain
Experience of winter
That is what will be real
The awesome presence of
Winter
Comes
Certainly

"Transition"

Embrace me with your rays
The warmth of summer
There is not
But the glimmer of memory
Sunshine of the fall
Still possesses

Hold me tight with the intensity
Summer sun brought
Even if not
A vestige of it will do

Fall is a waning of passions
That summer beheld
That winter will strip away

Transition
That is fall

"Longing"

—————— ∞ ——————

Fall
Come
Now
Enwrap me in your embrace
Tenderly
Lovingly
But passionately

Gentle gale
Ushering in the fall
Initiate me into your mysteries
Swiftly
Quickly
But patiently

Beautiful leaves
Marking the autumn season
Imprint me with your kisses
Falling
Sweetly
But firmly

Warm sun
Pressing on gentle pastures
Touch me with your affection
Caressingly
Smoothly
But intently

Fall
I cleave to you
As to no other
Longingly
Affectionately
And constantly

"Backing up"

———— ∞ ————

What was that?
Back up
Let's see what that was

Sitting in the driveway
In the corner
A glorious
Pumpkin
Carved
Formed
Jocular
Smiling
Like no care in the world

Glowing within
Brightly
Warmly
Emanates
Candle Light
Golden glow
Proclaiming to the world
It's Fall!

Aren't you glad that we backed up?
Yeah
Sometimes, it's worth it

"Why?"

It's always the same
Cars pass by
People give a cursory glance
Why are they in such a hurry?

Brightly shining
I
Sitting in the driveway
In my warm glowing
Proclaiming
It's Fall!

Wait a minute
A car's backing up
That's a first time
What'll happen?

A woman
And a man behind the steering wheel
Glancing through their windshield
A glow in the woman's face
A lover of the fall season for sure!

The guy
Not in love with the fall
But with her

"Love by Pumpkin Light"

What a lucky guy
I
Am!

Sitting next to
Woman
Beautiful
Glorious
Wonderful
That
I
Love!

Back up?
No problemo
Anything for you
I
Do!

Beauty of the Pumpkin
Glowing in all its
Glory
Does not compare

To the Love
Beside me
I
See!

Glad
To back up
Your beauty
Better
In the light
I
Admire!

"On the Window Sill"

Placed on the window sill
A quaint pumpkin
From last fall

Smiles
Eyes
Nose
Penciled in
A year ago
Slightly faded
Yet still visible

Sometimes forgotten
Other times beheld
Even held in my hand
Once in a while

The pumpkin
Rests satisfied
There
Not moving
A year later

Remaining faithfully
Although a little worn out
Placed on the window sill

"Snow Mass"

Snow Falling
Flakes of snow
So small individually
But collectively ubiquitous
Painting the world white

A flake of snow
In one's hand
Melts in fraction of seconds

Yet, snow covered
Over a long time
Flake after flake
Built up over time
Persistently
In aggregate
In collective sum
Seems not to melt
But stay the whole winter

Pressing one's hand on this snow mass
One cannot see the melting of snow
Even after few minutes

One does realize that one's hand is freezing
By the snow mass

A winter lesson?
In collective power

"Footprints in the Snow"

Footprints on the snow
Can they tell the story?

Small bird footprints hardly noticeable
Two sets of footprints

Could they belong to a mother bird and a father bird
Looking for food for their newly born baby birds?

May be they describe two bird friends walking together on the snow
Enjoying the new snow fall
I've seen birds fly in pairs before

Is it possible that a bird in love is chasing
Happiness?
See there the two sets of bird footprints seem to meet up

I wonder what kind of birds they are
I bet my high school physics teacher
The semi-professional birdwatcher could tell

Why didn't I go on that birdwatching expedition in high school?
If I did, I could probably tell at least what kind of birds they are

Even if I don't know the whole story behind those
Two sets of bird footprints

"On The Top of A Snow Covered Hill"

All around
Snow has covered the hills
Nothing underneath could be seen
The world has become white overnight

In the distance
In the whiteness of it all
I can see a small building

Seems like a pointed structure
It is also covered in the snow
Not completely
That it blends in with the snow covered world all around

What is that building?
Looking at the steeple
Colored in brown
And a cross above
It must be a church
On the top of a snow covered hill

"Spring Is Coming"

In the midst of the fiery winter
I can see a small piece of a green plant
Peeking out of the snow

Sunshine warmly seems to embrace that very plant
That stands tall in the midst of snow all around
Cold seems to hold no strength
With strength stands the short plant
Although barely pushing through the top layer of snow
It looks so tall and strong

With perseverance will come the bright springtime
Warmth will flow all over
Not only from the paucity of sunrays
But as radiant sunshine hugs the earth
The whole ground will emit warmth
And energy will overflow within
The small plant's whole being

Spring is coming
Hold on little plant
Spring is coming very soon

"Harkening back"

Under the overflowing tree I
Sit

It seemed like it was overflowing
Yesterday

Today it seems to be without the overflowing
Leaves

It is overflowing not with leaves but with
Snow

I realize that my pants is getting
Wet

It wasn't that way a short while ago in the
Fall

I remember the showering leaves beautifully
Colored

Red, orange, yellow, with different shades of
Green

But today all seems white all around
Everywhere

It is in the middle of
Winter

And here I sit as I feel the
Cold

I want to hold onto the memory of beautiful
Autumn

Perhaps hoping for an early
Spring

"A Lesson of Winter Rainfall"

Rain
Drip
Pour

Isn't it supposed to snow
Rather than this liquid precipitation we are getting?

Rain
Seems to be out of place in this season
Defiance by the autumn showers

Drip
Where's the soft inaudible sound of snow flakes?
Why the annoying sound so out of place?

Pour
At least it's coming down with passion
One should always do everything with a passion

A Lesson of
The winter rainfall

"Winter Truth"

The barren streets seem to haunt me as I drive through it
There is no green in sight
Just the orange yellowish dead grass and dirt in front yards
Trees totally bare of leaves
Naked and looking ashamed at being so
Perhaps feeling the winter cold rather than shame

As I drive I see how bleak everything is here
In the summer time with green foliage
It looked full of life
Like there was no worry in the world
And the place innocent and pure

But with the winter truth
Comes the revelation
Of the ugliness that was underneath
Cold and heartless
Without a soul
Life without a sense of purpose

In the bright bareness of winter
All is patently clear
This is a place not to garner affection and comfort

This is where one goes to experience pain and hurt
Summer foliage can no longer hide

"Spring Questions"

Why do I long for the springtime?
What awaits me?
Will I be happier with the new season?
Life will look brighter with spring flowers?
Perhaps allergies will keep me from appreciating them?
What's in springtime that brings hope and good spirit?
Is it warmth?
Is it more greenery?
The chance to play outside more often?
May be more strolls by the nice park?
Why do I long for the springtime?

"The Lone Tree"

Tenderly
Blows the gentle breeze
Rustling the lone tree
Leaves
Fluttering in the air
Branches slightly nodding

Warmed
By the faithful sun
Persistently stroking
Leaves
Basking in its rays
The lone tree stands tall

Climbing
Up the lone tree
A squarrel to frolic
Leaves
Held gently then tight
Plucked from their branches

Drip
Morning dew

Collected and dispersed
Leaves
Sucking in the morning energy
The lone tree basking in the autumn day

"Winds of the Passing Fall"

Like a whirlwind
Winds of the passing fall
Swirl and turn
Leaves helpless
Trying to cling on to the branches
Inadvertently
Hapless
Let go

The sky is filled
Colored
In Red
Orange
And Yellow

Leaves
Flying everywhere
Neither
Here or there

Leaves
Descend
Pell-mell

Knowing
Not
Where
They will land

Wanting
To hold on to the tree branches
But without a choice
They descend

Twirling
Dancing
Hopping
They make their way
Downward

Soon they will know
Where they will land
The place they will occupy

"*Where Have All the Leaves Gone?*"

———— ∞ ————

Where have all the leaves gone?
It seemed like yesterday
That I saw all those lush green leaves
Turn and change their clothing
Into gaudy and bright colors

Where have all the leaves gone?
The trees are now naked
Where is the beauty that marked them yesterday?
All I see are branches
Where are all the leaves?

Where have all the leaves gone?
Can changes come this quickly?
How did yesterday's fall splendor
Turn into today's shame?

How quickly things change!
How fleeting is glory!
How meaningless is yesterday's honor!

"Morning Sunshine"

How glorious is the morning sunshine!
In the crisp breath of morning calm
I behold
Through the densely colored
Fall leaves
A ray of sunshine
With hope and promise
Cutting through
Making its way
Towards me

How warm is the morning sunshine!
In the night
Tossing and turning
Having forgotten to turn on the heater
Too tired from yesterday's labor
To get up and figure out the new electronic heating equipment
Lying there
Knowing of cold
Clasping the winter comforter
Closer to my body
Now
The sunshine gently warms my body

How wonderful is the morning sunshine!
Brightly promising a hopeful day
Every day
Is
A new day
The whole land is brightened by the fall rays
The leaves glisten in their bright colors
The day is full of promises!
Life is beautiful!
There is always hope and promise!
How wonderful is the morning sunshine!

"A Beautiful Leaf"

Oh, those leaves!
I get into my car
And see my windshield
Filled with colored leaves
Fall has dropped on me

I need to get to school
There's a whole day
Awaiting me
Now
I need to get out
And waste few minutes
To clean out the windshield!

Oh, those leaves!
It's not like
Today's a typical fall weather
It's almost thirty degrees outside
I should have worn a thicker sweater
Who would have thought
In the middle of New England fall
One would need winter clothing

Ah, it's done
Now, I can get on my way
Work is waiting for me

Oh, how beautiful those leaves are
Those up there
On top of the tree
Yellow
Orange
Red

It's a pleasure to drive through such colorful
Landscape

And just in that moment of thought
Fluttered a beautiful yellow leaf
Hanging on my windshield wiper
And
I notice
How beautiful that leaf is

"Life is Like Fall"

Life is like fall
It experiences changes
It has its moments of glory
It is sometimes wonderful to admire
It is radiant

Life is like fall
It will surely pass
Youthful glory will be a memory
Beautify is ephemeral
A bleak winter is to be expected
Health, like leaves, will be stripped away

Life is like fall
One can appreciate the now and the present
Beautiful leaves can be adored
Praises for the glorious fall ambiance can continue
Photos, like a colored leaf between book pages, can rejuvenate

Life is like fall
It is what one makes it out to be

"Winter Beauty"

Winds are blowing
From the East
From the West
Perhaps from the North
I can feel them all around me

The winter winds circle all around
Warmth seems like a thing of yesterday
As I traverse the winter wonderland

Snow covered beautiful buildings
Hills dressed in Wedding White
Trees decorated in brightness of white snow
All seem so beautiful and wonderful

Winds blow
And I feel the chilliness of the winter cold
As I stand appreciating the beauty of winter
All around me

"Fireplace"

As I gaze into the flames
Of the warm fireplace
Thoughts drift
Towards yesterdays

I remember the night before a major test
Hoping for snow
In the morning seeing the world snow-covered
And school canceled
What joy for one in junior high school

Going outside
Making angels in the snow
Making snowballs
And sharing them in a friendly snow ball fight with neighborhood
friends
Making a snowman so big that it was taller than I was
And putting eyes nose and a smiling mouth on the snow creature
Even shoveling snow seemed like a fun exercise then

As I sit quite close to the warmth of the fireplace
And drift down the road to memories
I remember to add another piece of wood to the fire

And I resume my comfortable position
On the family chair
And resume a journey down another memory path

"Snow Everywhere"

Snow is falling
And falling
Almost pouncing the ground

Everywhere
All around
Snow
Snow
And more snow

Falling for minutes
Then hours
As if there's no end

Looking this way
And that
As far as my eyes can see
All I see is snow
Covering everything
Sparing nothing
All around it's snowing

"The Collective"

Walking among the bustle of the street
Losing myself in collective experience
Each adding to the summer afternoon din
Submerged within
I participate in corporate identity
Of being there
At that moment
In the midst of it all
Individuals walking about
Doing their own thing
But at that moment
All are united in the
Collective

"Summer Message"

The intensity of summer rays
Warms the core of my being
Heat rages within
And memories of the past winter fades
Sitting on the steps
Warmed by the sunny warmth
I contemplate the passions of summer
Raging within
Channeled through the fiery glow of the sun
Brightly shining within
Waiting to get out
Walking to convince
Those around
That summer warmth is the best

"*Summer Showers*"

Summer Showers
Pouring down
Tenderizing the parched
Earth
Eagerly desiring
The passionate water fall
Each raindrop
Tenderly massages
The body of earth
Bringing satisfaction
To the yearning
Of the core
To be filled
Satiated
Filled to excess
The boundless need
Yes
Oh yes
Elated
Fulfillment

"Road Ahead"

Taking a step forward
Onwards towards dusty paths
I forget that the road
That I am on
Is more dust-filled
Than the road ahead
Somehow
The visible streets
Ahead
Enwrapped by summer dust
Cloud my vision
Of the street
On which
My feet stand

"Summer Heat"

Looking to the right
Steering my vision to the left
I feel only the summer heat
And the visible
Matters less
Than the invisible humidity
My thoughts drift
Towards the waterfalls
Refreshing
Revitalizing
Rejuvenating
Cool sensation just beyond my immediate reach
Ready to satisfy
The thirst
Of summer heat

"Beauty of Life"

In the green pastures
I sit
And wonder
At the beauty of life
The living
As summer warmth
Sweeps across
And gentle summer rays
Sway the grass
Yearning after light

There is life all around me
Soaking in energy
And nature force
To endure
And prolong
Vibrant existence

And I think
About my life struggles
And it seems to be
Worth it all

"Withered"

Withered
In the midst of the field
Droops
A lone flower
Having weathered
Days of scorching sun
Holding on
Hoping for water
For rejuvenation
His friends
Other flowers
Nowhere to be seen
Already
Disappeared
Beyond recognition
Having
Withered

"A Shrill Cry"

A shrill cry
Rips through the summer calm
A sound
Filled with pain
Heaped on
Time after time
Demanding something
Perhaps justice
Testifying more
To atrocities
To inhumanity
Endured
And suffered
In silence
One with power
Abusing it
Thinking not of consequence
Without belief in a just God
Nor the truth of
What goes around comes around
The victim
Owner of the cry

Stands
As a testimony
And witness

"Over the Valley"

—— ∞ ——

Over the valley
And the hills
What lies beyond
As far as the eye can see
One sees only the desert
Desolate
Fruitless
Barren
No trace of life
Although there is living
No vibrancy
Nor effervescence
In the summer heat
All living
Stay
Stagnant
Inactive
Nothing moving
To and fro
Everything
Motionless
As if there is No
Life

"Tick Tock"

———— ∞ ————

Around the clock
Tick
Tock
Tick
Tock
The hand of time moves
With each tick
Time has passed
With each tock
Time past cannot be brought back
The sun chimes in
Moving along with each tick
The shadows follow with every tock
Inaudibly
Time moves
Swiftly
The present advances
And becomes the past
Future waits
But shortly
With each
Tick
Tock

Becomes
Present
Then past

"Road Before Me"

———— ∞ ————

In the middle of the road
I stand to contemplate
The road before me
And the path already past

Before me
I see sunshine
Brightly shining
Trees
Green as can be
Swaying gently back and forth
And merchants all along the road
It is a road
Indeed filled with happy people

Behind me
I only see the dust
That seemed not to have settled
No building
Neither of commerce
Nor of residence
No happy people there
Actually hardly one at all

I take one last look
Behind me
And resolutely
Easily
Walk towards the bright horizon
Before me

"Desire"

In the high noon
Of this day
I catch a glimpse
Of the beauty
That has captured
My heart
And thoughts

Thinking to give
Flowery pronouncements
I don't seem to be able to
But say
Only the most insensitive

Is it a defense mechanism?
Is it what women say?
What is it?
Yes
Fear of commitment

I wonder
At myself
As soon as words leave my mouth

There is a new side of me
I come in contact with
Desire
Foiled by my own words

Did I cause her pain?
I just don't know
But a small part of me
Hopes so
Because it means she care

What is this thing
That I am
An insensitive
Man
In search of a sensitive woman?

I catch myself
From my thoughts
After all
I can't let
My face
Serve as a mirror
Of my thoughts

I gaze into her eyes
There is no sign
Of hurt
Nor pain
But eyes brightly shining
Full of life

I find myself
Hurting
With desire

"Basic Human Rights"

Cowards are we
Who fear death
Or war
For the sake of dignity

To exist in humiliation
And accepting it
Requires virtue of
The lowest living creatures
Not worthy
To be called
Human

We are worse
Than dogs
We who
Do not fight for our
Basic human rights

World laughs
And mocks
Rightly so
Since we fear
When we must not fear

To protect
Our basic
Human
Rights
That only matters

"No One Wins in a War"

A wise man said
No one wins in a war
So why go to war?

Dignity
Was the resounding answer
Powers that be
Might take away
Possessions
And even positions of honor
But when basic human dignity
Is stripped
It is worth
Fighting
Even to the point of death

To die with honor
And dignity
As a human being
Is a noble thing
To live without
Basic human dignity
Which is everyone's right

Is not to live
But exist in a morbid state

A wise man said
No one wins in a war
To avoid war
Basic human dignity requires basic respect

"Those Beautiful Brown Eyes"

————— ∞ —————

Looking into those beautiful brown eyes
Glistening in the sun
Catching all the light
Shining
Exuding
Energy that is all around
Centered in those glorious eyes
I become absorbed
Mesmerized
By the magic
The mystery of it all
Almost helpless
I feel
Before the gentle gaze
I would do anything
Give up my whole kingdom
If I had one
I find myself confessing
To myself
And desiring
To profess
To her

"The Reddish Glow"

The reddish glow in her face
That the summer sun has wrought
What beauty it is
Enlightening
The dim chambers in my heart
I am sure
Almost positive
As the earth is round
As certain
As glowing coal
Passes its fire onto the cold coal next to it
That reaching out
And gently touching
The glow of her cheeks
Will inflame me
With everlasting glow
Just facing her
I am a believer
That there is life
Filled with glorious beauty
Transcending everything
Making world wonderful
Life is beautiful

"Lyre"

Stillness of the summer night
Is broken by violent barking of stray dogs
Aimlessly
Pell-mell
Must these dogs run
I hear them all around me
In the darkness
Although I cannot see
In the midst of all this
Peace is proclaimed
By a lone lyre
Dispensing music
Beautifully resounding
Like gifts on Christmas
It is freely
And joyfully given
By a modern Muse
Beautiful inside and out
With a pensive gaze
In tune with harmony
She is an instrument
Of salvation
In the midst of confusion

And darkness
The barking dogs fade
And in the moonlight
The tune of lyre
Graces the world
In which I find myself
The music fills my being
And my world glows
Refreshingly
As bright sunshine
After days of
Thunder and rain

"*Victory*"

———— ∞ ————

Victory is mine
There is assurance of triumph
In unity we cry out
Victory is ours
We will overcome
Different
We are
But united
We certainly are
For the common goal
Of freedom
And human dignity
We wage a moral war
Against those who want to oppress
The downtrodden and the disenfranchised
Those who abuse power
Will certainly have no footing
On this earth
Nor in the world to come
They are like dust
Scattered in the Judean desert
God is just

And humans created in God's image
Endure only justice
And righteousness

"For a People Oppressed"

A summer morning
Warm and dry
Sun shining brightly above
A new day of rejuvenation
Or another day of humiliation
For a people oppressed
And cannot liberate themselves
Hopelessly captured in history
And between the powers that be
Hopelessly enmeshed
Will a leader rise
And present leaders help
In the freedom of the downtrodden
Modern day
Social and economic slaves
Prayers to God
To aid in the freedom
Rose above from earth
To the heavens
It will come soon enough
As several times during the day
They resound throughout
Will salvation exist for this suffering people

Who cannot even demonstrate significantly
They oppose this oppression

"A Small Kitten"

A fading memory
Events in the past
Distant
Come rushing back
To me
As I look at a small kitten
Sitting among the flowers
Quietly the cat sits
Not uttering a meow
It looks so much like the cat
Who dwelled in that lovely home
Of even a lovelier lady
The time that we shared
Talking
Laughing together
And reminiscing about life
Life's philosophy
Shared
I remember it now
Even as if it were just yesterday
From the recesses of my past
To the fore of my present
I can even smell her hair

And the perfume that graced her body
And her tenderness

"A Worthy Human Goal"

In the annals of history
Or even in an invisible personal life journal
What will be written
About what we have done
To do good
To benefit humankind
To serve justice
Is it not worth it to participate in these virtues
Rather than do evil
Work toward injustice
And unrighteousness
Out of some clan loyalties
Some obligations to our in-group
To benefit only a few
Even if it means a little suffering for what is right
In the long run
Is it not worth the effort
And for personal conscience
To live for what is right
To act for the good of all
To be good
To be beneficial to humankind
To be doers of justice
This is a worthy human goal

"Oasis"

Oasis
In the middle of the vast dry desert
Spring of life
In the midst of nothingness and death
Blessed is he who finds it
Happy is she who partakes of it
So many search
Yea
Even comb the whole earth
But find only
Mirage
Filled with what is not
Happier are they
However
Those who make their own
Paradise
Here on earth
Wherever they are
Whether through toil
Or through imaginativeness
And creativity
Or through passionate love
And love making

Building hope
And living the dream

"Beauty of What Could Be"

Lying there under the early evening sun
With a lime stone chair as my bed
Surprisingly cooling my back
Next to me
I see ashes of previous campfire
That might have lit two lovers' faces
Under a full moon light
How beautiful it would have been
Surrounded by evergreen bushes
And colorful flowers
With a fragrance that moves one to sing
Love tunes
In the distance
Not too far away
Remains unlit candle
That brightly lit the loveliest face
Of the beautiful dame
Just the night before
How I wish she could be here
To share the summer breeze
And the beauty of what could be

"Meow"

Softly the kitten nears the transparent screen door
As I spot her so close
I pause what I do
And draw near to her
Carefully and slowly
Not wanting to startle her
Enjoyment of her summer walk
The kitten notices
With her feline alertness
In an effort to keep her near
I guess a name
Here, Kitty, Kitty, Kitty
No response
And I can see
She is ready to leave
In slight desperation
I call out
Meow, Meow
Hoping to connect with her language
I do not know what I have said
It is a language I only imitate
Seemed dejected
The kitten walks away

I remain
Not knowing
What I have said
In my meow's

"A Song"

In the middle of this summer night
Barely cooled by the evening breeze
I sing a song
At first softly
Almost inaudibly
Thinking about the one who has captured my heart
As I think about her radiant smile
Which fills the whole room
A cliché certainly true in this case
Tunes capture her loveliness
And I hear my own melodies
Rise in volume
And fill my room
Besides myself almost
I shout out the tunes
Identifying myself in the lyric's profession of love
And endless devotion
Compelled by my desire
To divulge to her
And profess to all
What I feel inside
Why can't this passion in tune
Convey itself in my conversations with her

At that moment
My joyous shouts of love
Embraces in tune
Feeling of pain
In already missing her
And in desiring her warmth

"*Independence*"

Independence
Freedom to be
Celebrating Independence Day
Remembering all that had to be given
Even precious lives
To be free
To have opportunities
Regardless of religion
Or racial background
Honoring the Independence Day
Is more than fireworks
And bar-b-que's
In our daily struggle
For the principles of freedom
And equal opportunity for all
Is festive re-enactment
Of the Spirit of independence
A true observance
Of Independence Day

"She Reappears"

I think about her
Her face stamped in my memory
At moments when her image seems to fade
She reappears
With her smiles
Glorious brown eyes
And tenderness
Feelings in me well up and overflow
And to press her firmly towards me
Stroking her cheeks
Those beautiful cheeks
Kissing her gently in her forehead
In her ears
Following down her tender cheeks
To her moist warm lips
Interlocking her lips in mine
Sharing the passion that we have for each other
At least my affection is genuine
Hoping hers is too
Love can be a wonderful testimony
Of the good of humanity
And the joy that we bring to each other

The physical pleasure of love
Is only a drop in the bucket
Of wonderful happiness

"To Behold Her Face"

———— ∞ ————

What a joy it is to behold her face
Even if just for a few moments
The magical glow of her bright face
And a smile that could march a thousand ships
Sweetness that is tastier than honey
The twinkle in her eyes that shines brighter
Yea, more illustriously than the stars above
Which shine in testimony of her beauty
As I look into her eyes
I want to hold her hands
Tightly in mine
Sit under the stars
And whisper in her ears
How beautiful she looks tonight
And the charm on her neck
Like a fragrant flower
Invites tenderness
Gentleness
How wonderful to shower her neck with
The most disarming of kisses
Saved just for her

"The Cat Again"

———— ∞ ————

I see the cat again
It seems to fancy me
Coming closer around the bend where I stand
Than before
I call out in the sweetest of tones
Meow Meow
Instead of coming closer
She moves towards the garden
Gently I pursue
Wanting to get closer to her
And to stroke her silky fur
I call out again in a softer tone
Meow Meow
The pretty kitten slowly walks away
But her steps seem to become slower yet
She stops and actually sits on the grass
And gently watches me
Does she want me to come closer
Or does she want me to stand where I am
In a short distance
I call out a few more meow's
I have the feeling she is warming up to me
And will be less shy in the future

"One Two Three"

One two three
From a distance
I see three figures standing in the middle of the road
I take my steps guessing who they might be
As I draw closer
The picture in the road takes a clearer form
I see before me
One sagacious
One beautiful
One brave
All kind souls
My eyes draw first towards the brown-eyed girl
With a gently smiling expression
One inviting and with kindness
I am afraid my tone in greeting will betray
My feelings for her
But another part of me wants her to see that
Her beauty makes me nervous
And my heart waits in anticipation
Of her love
We change greetings
She doesn't show any of her feelings towards me
I am left perplexed and confused

"Freedom Freedom"

Looking up at the sky
I cry
Freedom Freedom
I hear no answer
Only the twinkling of stars
Capture my eyes
And not even numerous stars
Only a couple stars

I ask myself
Where are all the stars
In the vast heavens?
Are they covered by clouds
A natural cause
Or pollution from all that are artificial?

Whether with numerous stars in the sky
Or with couple visible ones
Life goes on

With freedom
Or with servitude
Whether social

Political
Economic
Life continues

In songs of sorrow
Moments of happiness
Even with glimpses of freedom
Life exists

But just as I know that there are numerous
Stars in the sky
Even if I see only a couple shining brightly
I know that Freedom exists
And belongs to everyone
So I stand here
Before a seemingly empty sky
And shout
Freedom Freedom
I know that I am heard

"Romeo and Juliet"

She appears from nowhere
Perhaps from a world completely foreign
I realize her presence
With the fragrance of her being
In the warm summer day
In a room not too large
I sit next to a quaint beauty
Who just took her seat
I feel like she belongs there
And her agreement is in her body language
She leans closer towards me
And a piece of her clothing touches my arm
She leans further and her arm gently rests on mine
Quite invisible from the rest of the crowd in the room
Those who are preoccupied with their work
I look at her and think to start a conversation
With a few words of mine
I receive her bright smile
And an expression
Pretty but certain
That she understands not what I say
With a smile
Perhaps some sadness showing in my face

I bid her adieu
Which she seems to capture
Or perhaps it was time for her to go
She looks back
More than a couple times
Perhaps it is better this way
Do we need
Another tale of Romeo and Juliet
Two families torn in two
A story that ends in a tragedy
Happiness
Albeit intense
But short-lived
And sadness here to stay
And the story to be told over
And over again

"Wisdom Freely Given"

Knowledge is precious
But wisdom is more valuable
How wonderful wisdom is
Blessed is he who obtains her
And makes her his
A part of his essence
One that completes him
Together
He will be invincible
And always comforted
Being embraced gently in the bosom of wisdom
Stroking the beauty of wisdom
Their union will be called blessed
It is meant to be
What is more natural
Than for man to obtain wisdom
To wade through life's travails
And to enjoy all that is decent
And good
Beautiful shall you be called
Wisdom
And freely
Willingly

Joyfully
Will you give yourself
To one who toils to obtain you
Wisdom
You bring joy
And happiness
So your offspring
Begotten of a loving union
Will contribute to world's solutions
Love will abound
Peace will reign
Because wisdom freely gave herself
With fortuitous consequences

"Life Journey"

Lessons learned
Lessons taught
Life's a teacher
Experience a living exercise
People we meet
Those we will meet
Bring with them a whole experience of their own
Life comes
Life goes
Memories remain
Both good and bad
We think and we act
And we suffer the consequences
Or enjoy the fruits
Living
While learning from others
Brings meaning
Not only for problems avoided or solved
But in richness that comes through sharing
Life's journeys
That took an offbeat path
One that continued on a fast-track highway
Climbed over mountains and hills

Swam across the sea barely surviving
Parachuted down vast unknown skies
We learn as we listen
We love as we teach and share
In life we learn
In life we teach
Best students in life
Are not those who go the most direct path
But those who explore
And even live through the experience
Of others who went before
And are sharing the current journey
Called life

"Larger Than Life"

Dangling from a lanky tree
Small impressions
Of bright yellow
Flutter ever so slightly
All other colors
All around
Everywhere
Are earth-tones
Earth-tone green
That color the lawns
Even brown houses
In the surrounding
Have earth-tone quality
But the yellow leaves
Hanging carefree on that tree
Shine brightly
As if powered by a battery
Or a florescent light
Even people passing by
Have earth-tone coats
And pants
Cars parked along the street
Blend in within the earth-tone world

In the midst of dullness
Shines that tree
As small as it is
It seems larger
Than all the life around
Combined

"Benefit of Humankind"

Walking along the fall trees
Standing here
And placed there
I look to my right and behold a beautiful field of green
With no tree on its whole field
How many trees and flowers had to be sacrificed for this wonderful
field?
Ideal for soccer and other sports
Spanning beyond the field is a beautiful row of trees
Lined in no systematic way
But certainly colorfully adding to the beauty of the landscape
Providing a pleasant background for the soccer players
This view is a picture of sacrifice
Of trees
For the benefit of humankind

"Green Green Pastures"

Underneath a grandiose tree
Once so lusciously green
And like an umbrella
It provided me with a shade
Of greenery
A small world
In which to get lost
Under those leaves
I could sit and sip my coffee
And have a Sneakers bar as well
Thinking about all the wonderful things of the past
That walk along the Rose Garden
Gazing upon the waters from a quaint bridge
Sitting on the most beautiful patch of green grass in the world
Now I sit here
And I feel bare
Almost naked
As I look around me
And see open space all around
Leaves that have so plenteously covered the branches of the tree
Seem no more
All I see are bony tree branches
They even look thinner than before

I remain
Despite being self-conscious
Looking this way and that
Through the branches of the gigantic tree
I see what lay beyond the natural curtain of green
Blueness of the sky
With sun brightly shining
Seem to offer particular invitation
To tread down memory lane of happiness
I lean slightly back
As if there was support as with a comfortable sofa
While leaning on my hands
I tilt my head slightly back
And gaze through the view framed by nature's branches
I see the movement of a nice cumulus cloud mass
And think about the sheep that I saw in
Green
Green
Pastures

"Soul's Journey"

I raise both my hands
And extend them far above my head
Reaching out
Towards heaven
As if my physical extension
Lifts my soul to heaven
I tilt my head backwards
Looking forwards
To the heavens above
As if my gaze would pierce through the clouds
Providing a smooth and straight path for the soul's journey
Trees around me seem to do the same
Stretching forth towards the skies
Their branches piercing through the fall air
With leaves moving to and fro
As if to cheer the tree's efforts
I stand in quiet
With heaven's view clearly before me
And I can feel my heart beating
Reminding me that my soul
Is still here
Inside of me
I let out a sigh

Perhaps one filled with hope
For the future
May be my soul
Caught a piece of that beautiful heaven?

"Why Do We Stand Alone?"

In the midst of joys and sorrows
Sharing in the commonality of pain and pleasure
Suffering and hurt
Enjoyment and frolic
Why do we all stand alone?
Like those trees over there
Barely touching
Neatly placed side by side
But separately
Look at the lilies of the field
Flowers in a garden
Such as in a Rose Garden
Do they not stand close to each other?
Certainly touching one another
And even sharing each other's leaves
Thorns as well
How beautiful they all look
All closely gathered and exuding beauty
That is accentuated
In the multiplicity of numbers

"The Green Wall"

Streaks of green color the walls
Seemingly ancient walls
Certainly at least couple hundred years old
Made of aged stone blocks
Smoothed over
Into a fine masterpiece
The wall stands firm and solid
A source of comfort to the pedestrian
Who finds security in a sturdy wall along the walkway
Otherwise brown wall is imprinted in green
As colors of the leaves are shed over the wall surface
Even spurring new green life forms perhaps
Walking along such a wall
Imbued with life
I feel a sense of attachment
To the trees on the other side of the wall
I walk closer to the wall
Almost touching the green matter
Covering the wall
I could almost smell the green leaves
Belonging to the tree on the other side
Healthy trees with full and luscious leaves
Beautiful in its green glory

As I near the end of the beautiful wall
I slow my steps
Almost stopping
Because I do not want the beautiful wall
With wonderful trees on the other side
Just simply to pass me by
But again I take to steps
Throwing one last look backwards
At the glory of the wall
Then I gaze straight ahead
And I see trees all around
In front of me
And no wall to obscure my view

"The Tree"

---∞---

Lightly the gentle gale scratches my face
I turn around to see
Perhaps thinking that it was more than invisible wind
And I am met with a tree glorious and majestic
Colorful in the redness of its autumn leaves
It seems like yesterday that it was all green
Color of youth and innocence
I cannot imagine where all the time went
But there it is
Tree
Bright in its maturity
Heading towards the inevitable winter
When strong winds will blow
Perhaps all its leaves will fall
But even then
I know there will be beauty
In this tree devoid of its leaves
Snow will come
The tree will be covered in snow
With an appearance
More innocent and pure
Than its youth with green leaves

"Are They Chosen?"

Is there hope for my Palestinian child?
Does he look toward a lifetime of slavery?
Economic
Political
Social
At the hands of those
Professing to be God's chosen ones
Are they chosen
To enslave my child?
Are they chosen
To kill my children's friends?
Are they chosen
To ravage Palestinian homes?
Are they chosen
To rape my child's Palestinian wife?
Are they chosen
To deny my child opportunity for success
Just because he is a Palestinian?
Are they chosen
To be lord over us
And abuse my child emotionally?
Are they chosen
To lie about my child

And his Palestinian friends
To the world
And humiliate them?
Are they chosen to oppress?
What kind of God
Chose them to do these things?
Did Yahweh choose them?

"*Cast Aside*"

———— ∞ ————

Cast aside
Like a used rag cloth
Haagar
In her purity
Lost her opportunity to
Couple with her loved one
All because Sarah wanted a child
And Abraham did not complain
Of deflowering and
Sexually using Hagaar
The Jewish religion fully sanction
This sexual abuse
Hagaar was cast aside
Even left to die in the desert
After being sexually entered
Time and time again
By Abraham
Who abused his position of power
As a slave owner
Who treated Hagaar like a piece of property
When Abraham satisfied his sexual pleasure
And Sarah filled with disdain
Both of them

Cast Hagaar aside into the wilderness
To die
God was merciful
And saved Hagaar and Ismael
For Ismael is a blessed descendant of
Abraham
Despite Abraham's injustice and lack of social consciousness
As social and sexual abuser
God is just
Will God be just once again?
To the descendants of Abraham
As the Jewish State
Like Abraham
Willingly abuse and use Palestinians
As economic slaves
Then cast them aside
Into the desert to die
Will Yahweh come and offer them water
And provide salvation
Bringing justice for the Palestinians?

"We Too Are Abraham's Descendants"

In the raised hands of Moses
Ancient Israelites found victory
Who will raise his hands
For the righteous cause
Of human rights
And nationhood
Of the Palestinians
Who will Yahweh send
To bring freedom
For Palestinians
Who confess Yahweh
As their God
Will Yahweh hear
The cries of his children
The Palestinians
In their struggle against
The aggressive power?
Will Yahweh smite down
The oppressive State of Israel
As he promised
In the Hebrew Bible
To punish the oppressors
And those who abuse the weak

Will Yahweh keep his covenant
And destroy the wicked colonialist leaders
Of the Jewish State?
Is Yahweh dead?
Why doesn't he hear the cries
Of the oppressed?
Palestinians cry out
To Yahweh
Help us against the Jewish oppressors
We are also children of Abraham
We are also promised the Promised Land
Why do you
Yahweh
Exclude us from our inheritance
By allowing the State of Israel
To oppress us?
Yahweh
Keep your covenant
And
Liberate us!

"One by One"

———— ∞ ————

One by One
Steps of the oppressed is heard
Thinking that walking over a piece of land
Means reclaiming it
The Other
Walks the streets of Jerusalem
Some in solemnity
Remembering a child slain the day before
By the soldier
Of the ruling power
Another shouting words
Proclaiming freedom
As if his words might strike
The hardened hearts of the Oppressors
Some with stone in hand
In the spirit of Gideon's few
Dedicated to a righteous cause
Walking around the walls of the Old City
Will their walk
And shouts
Bring down the oppression of the Israeli State
As Joshua's group
Did in Jericho

Years before
Palestinians
Helpless before Jewish colonialists
Face heart
More hardened
Than Pharoah's heart
Yahweh has seen fit to harden Jewish hearts
To be merciless to Palestinians
But as Yahweh punished Pharoah
For enslaving the Other
Yahweh
If he is just
Will surely punish
The Jews and the Jewish State
For enslaving the Other
Cries for Justice
For Human rights
Is all but silent
Outside of Jerusalem
But Yahweh hears
The cries of the Other
The Palestinians

"Wipe Out Our Enemies"

Lord
Wipe out our enemies
The Gentiles
Who want to proclaim
The portion
You promised to Abraham
You seem extremely silent
That's okay
We have our tanks
And machine guns
And the Israeli made oozies
Just as effective
To realize the Promised Land
To exclude the Gentiles
From their right to this Holy Land
In our sense of righteousness
We'll kill the Palestinians
This is pleasing to you
Yahweh
The Holy One of Israel
We are your chosen ones
You are our God
Adoni is one

Blessed be the name
Ha Shem
Be exalted
Oh, Yahweh
May our sacrifice of Palestinians
Be pleasing to your sight
As we fulfill
The Divinely Sanctioned Hope
Of the Promised Land
To belong to His chosen ones
Lord
Wipe out our enemies

"*Make Noises*"

Make noises
With your voices
And instruments
Specifically prepared for this occasion
Shout out
With the loudest voice
When the name of Haman
Is resounded
In the celebratory reading
In Purim
In celebration of Yahweh's killing
Of our enemy
The Gentile
It is our right to fight and kill
Our enemies
Whether it is Rabin
The Jew who wanted to betray his fellow Jews
By considering Palestinians an equal partner in the Land
The Land Promised to Abraham and His Descendants
Or the Palestinian child protesting
Against an Israel soldier
We are the conquerors of the Land
It is Yahweh's command

Treaty made with the Canaanites
Or their descendants
The Palestinians
Displeases Yahweh
As Jews before us
Carried out Genocide against the Amalekites
In order to claim Israel as theirs
WE should fight
But genocide is so politically incorrect
Let's just oppress
Palestinians
And deprive them of their political right to nationhood
And use them as our economic slaves
Doesn't this fulfill the intent of the Law
For us
The Chosen People of God
Of Abraham
Isaac
And Jacob
To occupy the Land?

"Sitting Around the Table"

Sitting Around the table
Asks a child
How is this night
Different from any other nights?
The day when Palestinians
In the Promised Land were killed
Celebrating at the dinner table
A previous victory of Israelites over Egyptians
When Egyptians were killed
First born of all
Even the smallest
Cutest of babies
What is a father to say to his child?
That God liberated Israel
And brought them into the Promised
Land?
As the Holy Land was claimed
On the blood of Egyptian children
Yahweh
God of Israel
Is faithful
To deliver
His people

On the death
And blood
Of the Palestinian first born
To give the Promised Land
At all cost
To his chosen ones
Is it right that the Israeli Defense Forces
Kill?
What if the child asks this question at the same
Dinner table?
Should the father reply
This night is like the night
Of the first Passover
Yahweh kills for us
To keep his
Covenant
With His chosen ones
To give to Abraham and his descendants
The promised
State of Israel

"Ceremony after Ceremony"

Ceremony
After Ceremony
We remember the triumph of the chosen ones
Hannukah
We beat those Greeks
Passover
We kicked butts of those Egyptians
Purim
We killed that Haman
The enemy of the people of Israel
We are great
Yahweh is great
Each triumph celebrates the death of our enemies
Should we not institute a few more
Celebrations
That we could enjoy in our synagogues
Why don't we celebrate Yahweh's defeat
Of Nazis?
We'll add another ethnic group
To the list of people who were killed
For Jewish victory
How about the Palestinians?
They didn't oppress us

But we did incite them to violence
Kicking them out of their own homes
Oppressing them
Killing their children
Anyhow
They are Gentiles
Our enemies
Let us celebrate hundreds of Palestinians
Having been killed within
The past year
Victory for Yahweh
And His chosen people
Who else can we fight against
To claim victory for Yahweh
And for God's chosen ones
That is us
The people of Israel
We are all that matter
Yahweh
And His chosen ones
Gentiles exist to serve us
So it is with the Palestinians

"The Chosen People of the World Unite"

The chosen people of the world unite!
Yahweh is our God
And Adoni is one
We are His people
Wherever we are scattered
Be ingathered
To unite
To uphold the Promised Land
And the chosen people
Gentiles who try to lay claim to our land
Let us all unite
Under our Yahweh
Adoni is one
And fight and kill
To exclude them
From the portion
That Yahweh gave us
All the scattered of the House of Israel
Unite
Next year in Jerusalem
This is our everlasting hope

Cry of the Passover
Let the scattered
Be ingathered
And in the righteous warfare
Claim the Promised Land
Exclude
Oppress
Kill
Make sure all of Jerusalem
Belongs exclusively to us
It is our right
As the chosen people of God
Adoni is one
Let us stand together
To claim Jerusalem
At whatever cost
No other value is more important
Human rights?
That is only when people do not
Stand against us
The chosen people of God
The Holy Israel
Certainly
Palestinians
Have
No
Rights

"Eye for an Eye"

Eye for an eye
In this case
Palestinians
We suffered for two thousand years
We'll make someone suffer
Palestinians are as good as any
Who fit the description of
The Other
They are, after all, under our power
So we'll oppress whom it is easy to oppress
Oppress the Germans?
That's just too difficult
Germany is an economic powerhouse after all
We'll oppress the Palestinians
Who don't even have a state
Yes, we know
WE had to struggle for the Jewish State
But that's another story
Jews deserve a state
Palestinians don't
We are God's chosen people in the Promised Land
Palestinians are the Gentiles
Who have no right to our land

It doesn't matter that they lived here
For two thousand years
Yahweh promised this land to us
It is wrong to oppress God's chosen people
But even the Jewish Bible
Sanctioned Joshua to kill Gentiles
We are following only our divinely sanctioned right
Palestinians do not deserve their life
The Year of Jubilee?
That's only for Jews
Jews only had to set Jewish slaves free
Not Gentile ones
We are right
Because we are the chosen people of God
And we will not cease
To deprive Palestinians of their Land

"Capital Punishment"

Sanctioning the murder of their own political leader
Religious leaders have no problem
Reveling in the death of the Other
Like the Nazis before them
Who segregated the Other
To oppress
To kill
Leaders of Israel
Sanction
Segregation
Murder
With guns and tanks
With no conscience
In order to claim the Land
And kick out
And oppress
Inhabitants
Who lived therein
For thousands of years
Kill them
Cry out
Guns and tanks
As Israeli soldiers blast Palestinian towns

All of the world sit by
And watch
As the spirit of Nazis
Is kept alive
By Israeli soldiers
Who want to segregate
Oppress
And kill
Long live Hitler
Cry out
The guns and tanks
Of Israeli soldiers
Who will free the Palestinians?
Americans?
Like they did Jews from the hands of Hitler?
Who will save the Palestinians?
From the modern Hitler
Of Israeli Defense Forces?

"With Religious Banners"

With religious banners
And pious clothing
Killed a religious man
A peace seeking leader
One of their own
Whose only fault
Was seeing the Other
Possibly as same
Using religion
A religious man
Rose up
Sanctioned by his most reverent religious leaders
Whose permission was granted with religious legal stamp
In the square
Where people gathered
To proclaim peace in the Land
With the spirit of
Peace upon Israel!
Rose up a religious individual
Who proclaimed to represent all the religious Jews
And Yahweh too
He pointed his gun
Right towards the heart

Of the leader
Who had fought many battles on his behalf
And for his father before him
With a few rounds of gun shots
This law student
Killed not only the leader
His own leader
But dreams of peace that the leader represented
All in the name of Yahweh
And the Promised Land
Which he claimed
Belongs only to him and his kind
And those of his kind
Even
Who want to share
Deserve a death sentence
Sanctioned by Yahweh
What is this religion of Judaism
That he professes?
Religious banners
Of intolerance
And hate
In the Land
Which cries out for peace

"Crossing the Jordan"

Crossing the Jordan
Into the Promised Land
Fighting for an ideal
With remembrance
For past wrongs
Thinking of the forefathers
Wanting to reclaim the Land
Stand staunch
Freedom fighters
With only stones in their hands
Like David
Who hailed victory over Goliath
With slings and stones
Stand Palestinians
In the Land of oppression
Fighting for what is their
Right
Perhaps
As Rahab helped those who entered Palestine
Years before
Although she was not one of them
Palestinians may find
Among the very midst of their enemies

Those who stand for the just cause
And human rights
For which
The Palestinians
Fight
Freedom
Freedom
Is soon at hand
Stand bold
And reclaim your land
The basic right
Of all humans
To be
Free

"The Promised Land"

———— ∞ ————

The Promised Land
Stands far off
For the oppressed
Who voice their right
And stand for justice
With their very blood
They seek their human rights
God seems far off
Not granting the request
Of the stricken souls
In the Promised Land
Where is the Promise?
Those with power
And might
Abusing their authority
And power
With guns
And tanks
Continuing to enslave
Politically
Socially
Those who seek freedom
Killing voices

And bodies
Of Palestinian Liberation fighters
Barely armed with stones
And words
Where is Yahweh
That he not hears?
The cries of childless parents
Parents of children
Killed by machine gun bullets
Their only fault
That of being Palestinians
In the Holy Land
In which the oppressors
In the name of Yahweh
Kill
Maim
Hurt
And abuse
What kind of Holy Land is this?
Where Yahweh is an excuse for oppression

About the Author

———— ∞ ————

H. C. Kim is currently a Ph.D. student in Hebrew, Jewish, and Early Christian Studies at the University of Cambridge in the United Kingdom. He holds a B.A. degree cum Laude with a major in history and a minor in classical studies from the University of Pennsylvania in Philadelphia. H. C. Kim has two masters degrees; a M.A. degree in history from the University of California, Los Angeles, and a M.A. degree in theology from Fuller Theological Seminary. He has spent three years in Israel, researching in his subject area at the Hebrew University of Jerusalem, with the Goldsmith Foundation Scholarship, the Raoul Wallenberg Scholarship, and the Lady Davis Fellowship. Every summer, H. C. Kim returns to Jerusalem for research in his subject area. He has been featured in the alumni magazines of the University of Pennsylvania, the Hebrew University of Jerusalem, Fuller Theological Seminary, and the University of California, Los Angeles. H. C. Kim has delivered papers in academic conferences in the United States and Canada and has been invited to give special lectures in academic institutions in the Philippines, Germany, Russia, and Indonesia.

www.ingramcontent.com/pod-product-compliance
Lightning Source LLC
Chambersburg PA
CBHW022205050726
47590CB00002B/654